JAKE PAUL VS MIKE TYSON

How Mike Tyson, Jake Paul & Netflix won

Or did they?!

By Callum Coker

"As long as we persevere and endure, we can get anything we want."

Mike Tyson

ISBN 978-1-991338-43-3

Paperback.

First International Trade edition: November 2024.

A CIP catalogue record for this book is available from the National Library of New Zealand.

OTHER BOOKS BY CALLUM COKER

THE FREEDOM MESSAGE: PSALMS

THE FREEDOM MESSAGE: PROVERBS

THE FREEDOM MESSAGE: ECCLESIASTES

THE FREEDOM MESSAGE: GALATIANS

THE FREEDOM MESSAGE: EPHESIANS

THE FREEDOM MESSAGE: PHILIPPIANS

THE FREEDOM MESSAGE: GALATIANS +

FREEDOM POINTS

THE FREEDOM MESSAGE: PSALMS LARGE

PRINT EDITION

THE FREEDOM MESSAGE: PROVERBS LARGE

PRINT EDITION

Chapter 1

Let's set the stage shall we?!

It was built as a clash between generations, fame through social media and a world champion boxer of nearly thirty years ago, could a resurgent and seemingly ageless warrior like Mike Tyson knock out a punk like Jake Paul whose social media following alongside his brother Logan had catapulted them both into stardom.

The stage was set and the world tuned in, wanting a piece of what could be a new wave for Netflix in the entertainment industry, would they capitalize on a new market that was untested in the area of live sports in boxing. For those who hoped in a miraculous Mike Tyson comeback for the ages were bitterly disappointed as Iron Mike was left gasping for air after one round. The stunned silence of the crowd spoke volumes that this was in fact a stitch up for sports fans.

There was no miraculous comeback for Mike. There was no fan in the building who saw a great clash, as I watched from my seat in the living room of my couch I merely glanced over to my dad and said in a prior fight "I think we have seen the best two fights of the evening" and it was all downhill from there. So, what is the future for boxing in the entertainment industry. With what seemed like a boxing fight that was more scripted in the same ilk as WWE or WWF Where the show is preset and the winner pre-determined. Was this match fixed? I don't think so but what the consumer is after in sports at the highest levels is excellence, entertainment and the boxing match of the century fell well below expectations for consumers, they felt duped and rightly so. I came away from the boxing match wanting a rewind on my choice to be so pulled in by the hype. It was a truly great exponent of the concept of 'oversell and underdeliver'.

If Mike's fitness was better perhaps it would have been better, he was truly struggling with a knee issue or a leg issue of some sorts at 58 years of age this old battler from the slap heard around the world and not the Will Smith slap but the pre weigh in slap that singular slap showed pace, vigor, determination, where was that in the actual fight? How did the consumer get so well drawn in to the Mike Tyson comeback fairytale in hopes of a knock out to a punk thirty years his junior who was clearly in his athletic prime and what is the future for entertainment of this vintage as part of the streaming platform Netflix that relies on a global community of paying subscribers to buy in to their marketing and consume their content that is seemingly delivering on stories that are quite low on dialogic quality but deliver fast paced action.

What seemed like a slow-paced set of punches from Tyson after the first round that didn't connect at all in any manner continued into the latter rounds. The iron Mike Tyson of old was not present throughout the battle. Tyson was left outpaced and if he wanted to Jake Paul could have danced around the ring and not allowed any punching to take place purely to the athletic mismatch of a Tyson that couldn't move around the ring with any guile or pace to speak of.

I'm not a true boxing technician, I've had one boxing match in my life personally after a few beers at a mates place at University as we were prepping to watch an official boxing match that was labelled the fight of the century featuring Shane Cameron and David Tua, I liked the feeling of being in the midst of battle and wanted to knockout the guy I was paired to fight with, there was no dodging, looking for angles, I just threw left hook, right hook, right jab and didn't stop until the bell rang. All of my mates couldn't believe my strategy, but it worked. Tyson had none of that venom after a round, holding onto his gloves by biting showed him to be like a school kid, afraid waiting for his mommy to pick him up from school. This was a Mike Tyson nowhere near his prime he was entirely vulnerable to Paul as soon as that first round rang, he was out.

Chapter 2

Will this backfire 4 Netflix?!

Netflix is one of the largest companies on the planet. It has serious cash pouring into its business each month as subscribers pay their fee to get access to the content that they put up on their platform. In the case of the Irishman the bill for that over three-hour Martin Scorsese masterpiece that at times became a snoozefest was mega dough, did they get a return? Initially, there was Oscar buzz, big name actors from Hollywood and people watched it. Done, Next! That in many ways is the prescription of Netflix, 1. Work towards project, 2. Market heavily 3. Attract audience with big name stars and then 4. Onto the next project.

After the Logan Paul, Mike Tyson experiment proved to be an utter shambles, the viewer has every right to look at their dual subscription and entertainment prescription of Netflix and truly question. Is this worth my time? Am I receiving value for money? In a cost-of-living crisis globally many lower to middle income earners will be wondering is there true value in in this platform for me to invest in and rightly so! While Netflix will look at the viewers and head count initially of audience and viewership and see they have indeed made profit, the product was by all standards with regards to the main event a flop.

This fight proved to be two fighters that were now celebrities who turned back to fighting to maintain their celebrity. With mega dough in each other's back pocket did they make any new fans? I don't think so. Viewers turn away from mismatches and bullies and the Jake Paul – Mike Tyson experiment proved to be a disaster and very few people will ever watch that fight again.

They got people talking and attentive to their streaming service but the live product underdelivered for every metric except the first round. Mike Tyson struggled to get back into the match and the question is for Netflix, will this event backfire for a streaming service that has been so pivotal in millions of people's lives globally.

People are willing to pay for entertainment but the lack of quality content coming out for viewers must be concerning for the streaming giant with a lack of world class ideas and the economics of higher inflation, higher house prices and higher everything calls for swift and appropriate action at Netflix headquarters. Apple are competitive so is Amazon but Netflix has a brand stronghold in people's minds but if they do not adapt they will be overcome by market forces and competition that they will not be able to compete with in the long term. The kick on effects of an underwhelming live event for those who pay for Netflix that are predominantly in the middle-income bracket is a lack of satisfaction with the product on offer and a likelihood to not return to the product. Like when you attend a local restaurant, and you find the food or the service is not up to par you leave and don't come back. The exact same situation occurs in entertainment and Netflix is a lazy purchase that isn't questioned until you get a bad meal in this case the fight that will most likely be one of the most watched fights in history was an embarrassing watch for sports fans.

Mike Tyson's brand is built as a tough warrior but there was nothing tough about his efforts, people were concerned for him and rightly so while Paul looked strong and a bully ready to take on seniors who were not in their physical prime which is exactly what Tyson once was and in his prime Paul would have struggled to last a couple of rounds with Tyson.

If Netflix want to stay in the live sports game they need to adapt and they need to adapt fast. The costs of not getting it right far outweigh the positives as people can leave in their droves and look to other businesses like Apple, Amazon and YouTube to fill that void in their entertainment vacuum. There are so many choices on offer today and the market truly rewards excellence over quantity, they may have 1000 shows and movies to choose from but if there is not the quality to hook in consumers they could become a victim of their own behemoth.

To recover from this setback for Tyson will be about playing to his strength and that is leaning on authenticity and the truth and that is where we now turn our attention.

Chapter 3

Mike Tyson's rebranding after defeat

Mike Tyson the world champion knew fame and rewards of victory in the sport of boxing that very few people get to the highs he experienced they were high and the lows were low but what most people including me admire about Mike Tyson is his commitment to authenticity whether he is, was or will be in the valley or on the mountain top. He is likeable because he doesn't take a backward step, he presses forward through the questions of media with ruthless honesty.

I think he put everything he could into that fight vs Paul and wanted to dial back the clock so fans could step back into the ring with him one more time but when it doesn't go your way how does Mike Tyson restore his public image, the same way he has always done with ruthless, authenticity and honesty for someone who has seen serious lows and dramatic highs he has remained true to this one incredible quality of being himself. There is no doubt that Tyson was not in his peak physical shape but who would be at that age? With all his training the natural bounce back potential and ability to train and then fight against Paul was a fairytale that was really a disaster that was waiting to happen. It happened. Strength is exercised when you learn from defeat, and you also have a knowledge of your weaknesses. Does this hurt Tyson's image? Possibly but what is more important is that he remains true to himself and that is what people love about Mike is that he may be this tough boxer but deep down he has a massive heart for people and his family and that is why he has risen again post boxing as an incredible person for people to listen too for the wisdom that he possesses that is hiding in his simplicity.

Mike Tyson made a business deal but, in that business deal he put his whole heart into the battle that was to come and it didn't pay off in terms of results in the ring but it did pay off financially. Did he know what was going to happen? Probably - yes, he looked defeated as he was walking into the ring like he had been through something serious and the injury he suffered prior was going to have a bearing on this fight, but a warrior even wounded must still fight the fight and he did. To make the entire fight considering the hits he took from Jake showed that he was a man who was tough, battle hardened over decades and worthy of his titles that he had won a long time ago.

Tyson is a wonderful study of a person who has overcome so much and has an incredible gift for speed in the boxing ring with his hands and it was obvious that the speed he once had was now no longer present except for the first round and the slap that Jake took in the weigh in. For fighting to be a spectacle there needs to be an appropriate match up and this was always going to be a great match with a knockout within two rounds to Tyson or Jake or a drawn-out conflict where Tyson withstood punches and the pace of Jake.

Tyson immediately after the fight wanted another fight but I'm not so sure the fans would want to see that again I think a champion needs to know when to call it a day and when the fans leave the building before the speeches it's a sure sign that the champions days has a superb future well and truly behind him.

Chapter 4

Jake Paul… What were you thinking?!

Mr. Youtuber… Mr. tough guy, Mr. Pauly J or J dawg Pauly calling out Mike Tyson for a scrap who is nowhere near the same physical shape or chronological age as himself was punk like but it was a masterstroke for Jake Paul in marketing, building hype and the viewing public caught the intrigue of the question could a retired champion defeat a dude in his boxing prime with a solid record in the ring? The truth is for Tyson to win I think he knew that he had to do it in the first couple of rounds and if not then there was going to be a points decision in his opponents favour. He was out of puff within 2 minutes and the match was effectively over.

Mike and Jake made the deal of the century not the fight of the century. It was a Cinderella fight for the sports fans but the mechanics of the deal were clear cut before a punch was even thrown. Mike knew he needed to knock out Jake and early. It wasn't to be. Jake pocketed a lot more in cash for the exercise, he came up with the idea, he won the fight but did he win in the long run?

For sixteen minutes work that in many ways he breezed through, his reputation as a fighter did take a monumental hit. He dodged and weaved the first round but after that he was in total control of the fight and I think the crowd was silent because there was sorrow at the injustice of the match up and to the audience the match was already over as soon as they saw Tysons lack of co-ordination with the lower half of his body.

As a cricketer we still had a saying that you still had to put the bad ball away, when a bowler bowled a delivery that was not in the right place you still needed to put it to the boundary, score runs, tick over the strike. Jake Paul to his credit fought a fight that allowed him to defeat Tyson, he still had to put the bad ball away. Tyson didn't have a lot going for him in this fight in terms of fitness, his fatigue was obvious, but Paul still won that fight and showed he has many more fighting days ahead if he wants them.

Some athletes get knocked down and never recover, many do recover and bring the pains of their past experiences into the boxing ring with them, Paul and Tyson are fighters that use the pain of their past and dial into an endeavor that mimics the gladiators of old but for much more money and far less penalties. The blurred lines between Sport and entertainment and storylines that are tantamount to the drama series of Netflix and at the cinema are being tested in a way that has not been seen before and the advancement of our economies are being continuously trialed and tested in ways that benefits the athlete but is the product worth it for the viewer.

In the game of golf we see the emergence of LIV golf being a disruptor to the PGA tour we now see the pay per view model of boxing being part of the business model of Netflix as they try to capture chunks of the market share that are available in the sport of Boxing. The market is curious, the fans are curious but has the market been hurt by the product that they may not want to try again?

The Beauty of McDonald's is that it produces burgers time and time again that are consistent, they all have a similar McDonald's taste but no matter which part of the world you are in you can trust the product to be delivered to the customer in a way that builds trust and is not to costly and not that you feel you are having your life savings ripped from you. To get the business model right between fame and performance for this new product is a delicate balancing act that requires a lot of skill, finesse and fortitude in the sport of Boxing. This new generation wants entertainment in bite sized punchy form. The game of cricket has adapted to this new market with T20 cricket building a fan base that caters to this new generation of people who have less time to be entertained so known celebrities in a boxing ring for a short amount of time is an intriguing business model if delivered well.

Can they continue to invest in this business model Netflix? Yes, most definitely but fans want the match ups to be fairer, they want a spectacle. In New Zealand there was an event called the fight for life that was a roaring success whereby celebs within the New Zealand context fought one another for charity but that event no longer takes place but it was successful at the time.

Seeing sports stars cross codes is nothing new we have seen Michael Jordan try baseball midway through a successful basketball career, we have seen Sonny Bill Williams code swap professionally between boxing, rugby league and rugby union. He was successful in each until he got knocked out and has transitioned into commentary as well. In many ways his pursuit of excellence in each sport has been inspirational and he was no doubt a role model for many young kids growing up in Australia and New Zealand where his sports careers flourished.

So, what about Boxers who find themselves in the boxing ring and are struggling to let go, that want to fight, what then – where do they go? Jake has gone about his career in the opposite way to Mike Tyson, Jake got famous primarily through YouTube and then through YouTube he had a fan base for his boxing career, although the lines between the two of those pursuits is somewhat blurred as well there is truth that if you want to go after something you can and he has found solace in purpose in both. Boxing his way out of his demons, his struggles, his fears. Like Alex Honnold, he is most happy when climbing in his case boxing.

Jake has direction inside the boxing ring. A legitimate fighter - he most definitely is! But he needs to bring the crowd back into his camp, nobody in that crowd wanted Jake Paul to win maybe because the fight was so completely stacked in his favour but so many wanted to see a fair fight and contest that would be legendary.

Paul will recover and move on to his next bout, a win is a win and that is efficient cargo in the sporting world. We need champions to celebrate not villains who beat up old dudes and that will be the question on how to rebrand for the Paul team.

How do Netflix get the formula right in a market that is blurring the lines between entertainment and sport? That is the question we now turn too in the next chapter.

Chapter 5

The rebrand mix for Jake Paul and Netflix

Will they want another fight? If Jake and Mike Tyson said they want a rematch would the world show up? I don't think so, the stadium would be empty, the viewers would be nil. The home run had already taken place for both with the fans left empty. They didn't deserve this so how does Netflix pivot from the fallout of what was by all accounts a total disaster in the entertainment and boxing world.

Jake needs to fight opponents that are in his age range and have a bit of spice to the encounter, a celebrity turned boxer fight is a possibility but there needs to be a true fight again for this guy to be taken seriously in the boxing world and by his fans.

Many people over in the United States would want another champion in their midst and they will only feel deflated if the boxing matchups that are on offer for celebrity turned boxer fights resemble the world of WWE. If that is the case why doesn't Jake take a go at wrestling or even better call out a guy like John Cena or a Dwayne the Rock Johnson? Or maybe Zac Efron? In terms of boxing he won't be taken seriously but as a business model there is scope for fights that people want. In the WWE world there is a bad guy and a good guy, you could market the good guy and the bad guy in the boxing world. Jake just needs to find an opponent of skill who is disliked more than him post the Mike Tyson scrap. Mike didn't lose that fight we all did by watching it and in many ways this book is really a cathartic look into the battle to figure out how the viewer got duped by the entire event? Why did we fall for the marketing when the outcome was so obvious before each fighter stepped into the ring to make their first punch.

We need a storyline that makes sense. I think the code swap between WWE or Kickboxing and boxing is intriguing, someone like Andrew Tate would be an intriguing matchup for Paul or another Youtuber who connects with a generation that is much – much closer in age to Jake.

Netflix can't make this same mistake again, the undercards of the night were far superior in their entertainment value and they produced terrific value for the consumer. Not everyone can get the formula right the first time in a new venture and they need to make sure that if they want to enter the live sports arena that they get matchups that are appealing and fair. The lopsided Jake Paul and Mike Tyson match was ugly, it wasn't fair on the consumer and the consumer will revolt if it continues.

Mike Tyson wasn't fit. plain and simple. He can't fight at that level again unless there is rigorous testing that ensures his speed is back, It wasn't and it will prove costly for any fight promoter if he wants another scrap. Mike is a personality that attracts attention and his post boxing life has been extremely successful because he has been so authentic.

Mike Tyson, won, Jake Paul won, and Netflix won temporarily but if the consumer is not respected they will lose their reputations and that is worth much more than the million of bucks now stuffed into each of their back pockets. Or did they lose and we the consumer won in the long run? only time will tell.

Chapter 6

Conclusion

The fight is over

the winner has won

but u the consumer are back 2 square 1

cud we have ever imagined cud have we ever reasoned that a fight between a champion and YouTuber b worse 4 only 1.

Today is not tomorrow nd 2morrow is not 2day but a place in my heart will long for a new day

wen a new champ arrives and a fair fight emerges, crowds will get what they deserve a fight for the ages.

ABOUT THE AUTHOR

Callum Coker is a keen observer of sport playing both Rugby and Cricket in his native country of New Zealand throughout his youth, he holds a Bachelor of Sport and Exercise and plays golf when he can. He is also the Author of THE FREEDOM MESSAGE a modern-day translation of the Bible that reimagines the world of the Bible like never b4.